DOVER · THRIFT · EDITIONS

# Best Poems of the Brontë Sisters

## EMILY, ANNE AND CHARLOTTE BRONTË

DOVER PUBLICATIONS, INC.
Mineola, New York

# DOVER THRIFT EDITIONS

GENERAL EDITOR: STANLEY APPELBAUM
EDITOR OF THIS VOLUME: SUSAN L. RATTINER

*Bibliographical Note*

This Dover edition, first published in 1997, is a new selection of 47 poems by Emily, Anne and Charlotte Brontë, reprinted from standard texts. A new Note has been specially prepared for this edition.

*Library of Congress Cataloging-in-Publication Data*

Brontë, Emily, 1818–1848.
   Best poems of the Brontë Sisters / Emily, Anne, and Charlotte Brontë.
         p.      cm. — (Dover thrift editions)
      ISBN 0-486-29529-X (pbk.)
      1. English poetry — Women authors. 2. English poetry — 19th century. I. Brontë, Anne, 1820–1849. II. Brontë, Charlotte, 1816–1855. III. Title. IV. Series.
PR4166.B76   1997
821'.808 — dc20                                                             96-38774
                                                                                       CIP

Manufactured in the United States of America
Dover Publications, Inc., 31 East 2nd Street, Mineola, N.Y. 11501

# Note

THE THREE BRONTË SISTERS, Charlotte, Emily Jane and Anne, have earned distinction for their novels and poems. The Brontë parents, Patrick and Maria Branwell, had six children: Maria (1813–1825), Elizabeth (1814–1825), Charlotte (1816–1855), Patrick Branwell (1817–1848), Emily Jane (1818–1848) and Anne (1820–1849). Both parents were intelligent writers, and encouraged their children to share an appreciation of writing. The father, Patrick, was a clergyman, and the mother, Maria Branwell, died of cancer when her youngest child was only a year old. After Mrs. Brontë died, her sister, Elizabeth Branwell, arrived to help raise her sister's children. However, the children did not receive the nurturing from her that their mother had provided. The Brontë children retreated into an imaginary world, inventing many stories and tales. Emily and Anne collaborated on stories and poems all of which involved a make-believe island called Gondal, continuing this fantasy even into their twenties.

Patrick Brontë sent his four oldest daughters to Cowan Bridge School, which led to Maria and Elizabeth's typhoid fever, tuberculosis and subsequent death. This school also played an important role in furnishing a setting for Charlotte's novel *Jane Eyre*. After the death of their two eldest sisters in 1825, Charlotte and Emily were brought home to be educated with Anne and their brother Branwell.

Of the three sisters, Emily is considered by critics to be the best poet, conveying a myriad of intense emotions in her poetry. However, Emily was an extremely private individual and had to be coaxed by Charlotte into submitting her poetry to be published. Insisting on anonymity, the Brontës published *Poems by Currer, Ellis, and Acton Bell* in 1846. These pseudonyms for Charlotte, Emily and Anne, respectively, were intentionally ambiguous to conceal their gender. The reason behind this camouflage was twofold; the sisters wanted to maintain their privacy, and, at the same time, escape the prejudices that would surely arise from being classified as "women." The book of poems sold only two copies, and the Brontës began writing novels.

Charlotte completed her most famous work, *Jane Eyre*, in 1847. This was her second novel; her first was *The Professor*, which was published after her death. *Shirley* (1849) and *Villette* (1853) are among her lesser known novels. In 1854, Charlotte married Arthur Bell Nicholls, her father's curate. Emily published *Wuthering Heights* in 1847, still refusing to discard her pseudonym. Anne's novels included *Agnes Grey* (1847) and *The Tenant of Wildfell Hall* (1848).

In 1848 Branwell Brontë died from alcoholism and opium addiction. Soon after Branwell's death, Emily contracted tuberculosis and died on December 19, 1848. Afflicted with the same disease that claimed the rest of her siblings, Anne, too, died of tuberculosis on May 28, 1849. In 1850 Charlotte published a new edition of *Wuthering Heights and Agnes Grey* with a "Biographical Notice" of her sisters. Charlotte died in 1855, at the age of thirty-nine.

The present edition is comprised of a selection of poems written by Emily, Anne and Charlotte Brontë, many of which first appeared in the 1846 edition of *Poems by Currer, Ellis, and Acton Bell* (published in London by Aylott and Jones). The 47 poems printed here are arranged by poet and reflect the sequence of the 1846 edition.

# Contents

## Charlotte Brontë (1816–1855)

## Emily Brontë (1818–1848)

## Anne Brontë (1820–1849)

# CHARLOTTE BRONTË

## The Letter

What is she writing? Watch her now,
  How fast her fingers move!
How eagerly her youthful brow
  Is bent in thought above!
Her long curls, drooping, shade the light,
  She puts them quick aside,
Nor knows, that band of crystals bright,
  Her hasty touch untied.
It slips adown her silken dress,
  Falls glittering at her feet;
Unmarked it falls, for she no less
  Pursues her labour sweet.

The very loveliest hour that shines,
  Is in that deep blue sky;
The golden sun of June declines,
  It has not caught her eye.
The cheerful lawn, and unclosed gate,
  The white road, far away,
In vain for her light footsteps wait,
  She comes not forth to-day.
There is an open door of glass
  Close by that lady's chair,
From thence, to slopes of mossy grass,
  Descends a marble stair.

Tall plants of bright and spicy bloom
  Around the threshold grow;
Their leaves and blossoms shade the room,
  From that sun's deepening glow.
Why does she not a moment glance
  Between the clustering flowers,
And mark in heaven the radiant dance
  Of evening's rosy hours?
O look again! Still fixed her eye,
  Unsmiling, earnest, still,
And fast her pen and fingers fly,
  Urged by her eager will.

Her soul is in th' absorbing task;
    To whom, then, doth she write?
Nay, watch her still more closely, ask
    Her own eyes' serious light;
Where do they turn, as now her pen
    Hangs o'er th' unfinished line?
Whence fell the tearful gleam that then
    Did in their dark spheres shine?
The summer-parlour looks so dark,
    When from that sky you turn,
And from th' expanse of that green park,
    You scarce may aught discern.

Yet o'er the piles of porcelain rare,
    O'er flower-stand, couch, and vase,
Sloped, as if leaning on the air,
    One picture meets the gaze.
'Tis there she turns; you may not see
    Distinct, what form defines
The clouded mass of mystery
    Yon broad gold frame confines.
But look again; inured to shade
    Your eyes now faintly trace
A stalwart form, a massive head,
    A firm, determined face.

Black Spanish locks, a sunburnt cheek,
    A brow high, broad, and white,
Where every furrow seems to speak
    Of mind and moral might.
Is that her god? I cannot tell;
    Her eye a moment met
Th' impending picture, then it fell
    Darkened and dimmed and wet.
A moment more, her task is done,
    And sealed the letter lies;
And now, towards the setting sun
    She turns her tearful eyes.

Those tears flow over, wonder not,
    For by the inscription, see
In what a strange and distant spot

Her heart of hearts must be!
Three seas and many a league of land
    That letter must pass o'er,
E'er read by him to whose loved hand
    'Tis sent from England's shore.
Remote colonial wilds detain
    Her husband, loved though stern;
She, 'mid that smiling English scene,
    Weeps for his wished return.

## Regret

Long ago I wished to leave
"The house where I was born;"
Long ago I used to grieve,
My home seemed so forlorn.
In other years, its silent rooms
Were filled with haunting fears;
Now, their very memory comes
O'ercharged with tender tears.

Life and marriage I have known,
Things once deemed so bright;
Now, how utterly is flown
Every ray of light!
'Mid the unknown sea of life
I no blest isle have found;
At last, through all its wild wave's strife,
My bark is homeward bound.

Farewell, dark and rolling deep!
Farewell, foreign shore!
Open, in unclouded sweep,
Thou glorious realm before!
Yet, though I had safely pass'd
That weary, vexed main,
One loved voice, through surge and blast,
Could call me back again.

Though the soul's bright morning rose
O'er Paradise for me,
William! even from Heaven's repose
I'd turn, invoked by thee!
Storm nor surge should e'er arrest
My soul, exulting then:
All my heaven was once thy breast,
Would it were mine again!

# Presentiment

"Sister, you've sat there all the day,
    Come to the hearth awhile;
The wind so wildly sweeps away,
    The clouds so darkly pile.
That open book has lain, unread,
    For hours upon your knee;
You've never smiled nor turned your head
    What can you, sister, see?"

"Come hither, Jane, look down the field;
    How dense a mist creeps on!
The path, the hedge, are both concealed,
    Ev'n the white gate is gone;
No landscape through the fog I trace,
    No hill with pastures green;
All featureless is nature's face,
    All masked in clouds her mien.

"Scarce is the rustle of a leaf
    Heard in our garden now;
The year grows old, its days wax brief,
    The tresses leave its brow.
The rain drives fast before the wind,
    The sky is blank and grey;
O Jane, what sadness fills the mind
    On such a dreary day!"

"You think too much, my sister dear;
    You sit too long alone;
What though November days be drear?

Full soon will they be gone.
I've swept the hearth, and placed your chair,
   Come, Emma, sit by me;
Our own fireside is never drear,
Though late and wintry wane the year,
   Though rough the night may be."

"The peaceful glow of our fireside
   Imparts no peace to me:
My thoughts would rather wander wide
   Than rest, dear Jane, with thee.
I'm on a distant journey bound,
   And if, about my heart,
Too closely kindred ties were wound,
   'T would break when forced to part.

" 'Soon will November days be o'er:'
   Well have you spoken, Jane:
My own forebodings tell me more,
For me, I know by presage sure,
   They'll ne'er return again.
Ere long, nor sun nor storm to me
   Will bring or joy or gloom;
They reach not that Eternity
   Which soon will be my home."

Eight months are gone, the summer sun
   Sets in a glorious sky;
A quiet field, all green and lone,
   Receives its rosy dye.
Jane sits upon a shaded stile,
   Alone she sits there now;
Her head rests on her hand the while,
   And thought o'ercasts her brow.

She's thinking of one winter's day,
   A few short months ago,
When Emma's bier was borne away
   O'er wastes of frozen snow.
She's thinking how that drifted snow
   Dissolved in spring's first gleam,

And how her sister's memory now
    Fades, even as fades a dream.

The snow will whiten earth again,
    But Emma comes no more;
She left, 'mid winter's sleet and rain,
    This world for Heaven's far shore.
On Beulah's hills she wanders now,
    On Eden's tranquil plain;
To her shall Jane hereafter go,
    She ne'er shall come to Jane!

## The Teacher's Monologue

The room is quiet, thoughts alone
People its mute tranquillity;
The yoke put off, the long task done, —
I am, as it is bliss to be,
Still and untroubled. Now, I see,
For the first time, how soft the day
O'er waveless water, stirless tree,
Silent and sunny, wings its way.
Now, as I watch that distant hill,
So faint, so blue, so far removed,
Sweet dreams of home my heart may fill,
That home where I am known and loved:
It lies beyond; yon azure brow
Parts me from all Earth holds for me;
And, morn and eve, my yearnings flow
Thitherward tending, changelessly.
My happiest hours, aye! all the time,
I love to keep in memory,
Lapsed among moors, ere life's first prime
Decayed to dark anxiety.

Sometimes, I think a narrow heart
Makes me thus mourn those far away,
And keeps my love so far apart
From friends and friendships of to-day;
Sometimes, I think 'tis but a dream
I treasure up so jealously,

All the sweet thoughts I live on seem
To vanish into vacancy:
And then, this strange, coarse world around
Seems all that's palpable and true;
And every sight, and every sound,
Combines my spirit to subdue
To aching grief, so void and lone
Is Life and Earth — so worse than vain,
The hopes that, in my own heart sown,
And cherished by such sun and rain
As Joy and transient Sorrow shed,
Have ripened to a harvest there:
Alas! methinks I hear it said,
"Thy golden sheaves are empty air."

All fades away; my very home
I think will soon be desolate;
I hear, at times, a warning come
Of bitter partings at its gate;
And, if I should return and see
The hearth-fire quenched, the vacant chair;
And hear it whispered mournfully,
That farewells have been spoken there,
What shall I do, and whither turn?
Where look for peace? When cease to mourn?

'Tis not the air I wished to play,
    The strain I wished to sing;
My wilful spirit slipped away
    And struck another string.
I neither wanted smile nor tear,
    Bright joy nor bitter woe,
But just a song that sweet and clear,
    Though haply sad, might flow.

A quiet song, to solace me
    When sleep refused to come;
A strain to chase despondency,
    When sorrowful for home.
In vain I try; I cannot sing;
    All feels so cold and dead;

No wild distress, no gushing spring
    Of tears in anguish shed;

But all the impatient gloom of one
    Who waits a distant day,
When, some great task of suffering done,
    Repose shall toil repay.
For youth departs, and pleasure flies,
    And life consumes away,
And youth's rejoicing ardour dies
    Beneath this drear delay;

And Patience, weary with her yoke,
    Is yielding to despair,
And Health's elastic spring is broke
    Beneath the strain of care.
Life will be gone ere I have lived;
    Where now is Life's first prime?
I've worked and studied, longed and grieved,
    Through all that rosy time.

To toil, to think, to long, to grieve, —
    Is such my future fate?
The morn was dreary, must the eve
    Be also desolate?
Well, such a life at least makes Death
    A welcome, wished-for friend;
Then, aid me, Reason, Patience, Faith,
    To suffer to the end!

## Passion

Some have won a wild delight,
    By daring wilder sorrow;
Could I gain thy love to-night,
    I'd hazard death to-morrow.

Could the battle-struggle earn
    One kind glance from thine eye,
How this withering heart would burn,
    The heady fight to try!

Welcome nights of broken sleep,
    And days of carnage cold,
Could I deem that thou wouldst weep
    To hear my perils told.

Tell me, if with wandering bands
    I roam full far away,
Wilt thou, to those distant lands,
    In spirit ever stray?

Wild, long, a trumpet sounds afar;
    Bid me — bid me go
Where Seik and Briton meet in war,
    On Indian Sutlej's flow.

Blood has dyed the Sutlej's waves
    With scarlet stain, I know;
Indus' borders yawn with graves,
    Yet, command me go!

Though rank and high the holocaust
    Of nations, steams to heaven,
Glad I'd join the death-doomed host,
    Were but the mandate given.

Passion's strength should nerve my arm,
    Its ardour stir my life,
Till human force to that dread charm
Should yield and sink in wild alarm,
    Like trees to tempest-strife.

If, hot from war, I seek thy love,
    Darest thou turn aside?
Darest thou, then, my fire reprove,
    By scorn, and maddening pride?

No — my will shall yet control
    Thy will, so high and free,
And love shall tame that haughty soul —
    Yes — tenderest love for me.

I'll read my triumph in thine eyes,
   Behold, and prove the change;
Then leave, perchance, my noble prize,
   Once more in arms to range.

I'd die when all the foam is up,
   The bright wine sparkling high;
Nor wait till in the exhausted cup
   Life's dull dregs only lie.

Then Love thus crowned with sweet reward,
   Hope blest with fulness large,
I'd mount the saddle, draw the sword,
   And perish in the charge!

## Preference

Not in scorn do I reprove thee,
Not in pride thy vows I waive,
But, believe, I could not love thee,
Wert thou prince, and I a slave.
These, then, are thine oaths of passion?
This, thy tenderness for me?
Judged, even, by thine own confession,
Thou art steeped in perfidy.
Having vanquished, thou wouldst leave me!
Thus I read thee long ago;
Therefore, dared I not deceive thee,
Even with friendship's gentle show.
Therefore, with impassive coldness
Have I ever met thy gaze;
Though, full oft, with daring boldness,
Thou thine eyes to mine didst raise.
Why that smile? Thou now art deeming
This my coldness all untrue, —
But a mask of frozen seeming,
Hiding secret fires from view.
Touch my hand, thou self-deceiver;
Nay — be calm, for I am so:
Does it burn? Does my lip quiver?
Has mine eye a troubled glow?

Canst thou call a moment's colour
To my forehead — to my cheek?
Canst thou tinge their tranquil pallor
With one flattering, feverish streak?
Am I marble? What! no woman
Could so calm before thee stand?
Nothing living, sentient, human,
Could so coldly take thy hand?
Yes — a sister might, a mother:
My good-will is sisterly:
Dream not, then, I strive to smother
Fires that inly burn for thee.
Rave not, rage not, wrath is fruitless,
Fury cannot change my mind;
I but deem the feeling rootless
Which so whirls in passion's wind.
Can I love? Oh, deeply — truly —
Warmly — fondly — but not thee;
And my love is answered duly,
With an equal energy.
Wouldst thou see thy rival? Hasten,
Draw that curtain soft aside,
Look where yon thick branches chasten
Noon, with shades of eventide.
In that glade, where foliage blending
Forms a green arch overhead,
Sits thy rival thoughtful bending
O'er a stand with papers spread —
Motionless, his fingers plying
That untired, unresting pen;
Time and tide unnoticed flying,
There he sits — the first of men!
Man of conscience — man of reason;
Stern, perchance, but ever just;
Foe to falsehood, wrong, and treason,
Honour's shield, and virtue's trust!
Worker, thinker, firm defender
Of Heaven's truth — man's liberty;
Soul of iron — proof to slander,
Rock where founders tyranny.
Fame he seeks not — but full surely
She will seek him, in his home;

This I know, and wait securely
For the atoning hour to come.
To that man my faith is given,
Therefore, soldier, cease to sue;
While God reigns in earth and heaven,
I to him will still be true!


## Parting.

There's no use in weeping,
Though we are condemned to part:
There's such a thing as keeping
A remembrance in one's heart:

There's such a thing as dwelling
On the thought ourselves have nurs'd,
And with scorn and courage telling
The world to do its worst.

We'll not let its follies grieve us,
We'll just take them as they come;
And then every day will leave us
A merry laugh for home.

When we've left each friend and brother,
When we're parted wide and far,
We will think of one another,
As even better than we are.

Every glorious sight above us,
Every pleasant sight beneath,
We'll connect with those that love us,
Whom we truly love till death!

In the evening, when we're sitting
By the fire perchance alone,
Then shall heart with warm heart meeting,
Give responsive tone for tone.

We can burst the bonds which chain us,
Which cold human hands have wrought,
And where none shall dare restrain us
We can meet again, in thought.

So there's no use in weeping,
Bear a cheerful spirit still;
Never doubt that Fate is keeping
Future good for present ill!

## Winter Stores

We take from life one little share,
    And say that this shall be
A space, redeemed from toil and care,
    From tears and sadness free.

And, haply, Death unstrings his bow
    And Sorrow stands apart,
And, for a little while, we know
    The sunshine of the heart.

Existence seems a summer eve,
    Warm, soft, and full of peace;
Our free, unfettered feelings give
    The soul its full release.

A moment, then, it takes the power,
    To call up thoughts that throw
Around that charmed and hallowed hour,
    This life's divinest glow.

But Time, though viewlessly it flies,
    And slowly, will not stay;
Alike, through clear and clouded skies,
    It cleaves its silent way.

Alike the bitter cup of grief,
    Alike the draught of bliss,
Its progress leaves but moment brief
    For baffled lips to kiss.

The sparkling draught is dried away,
　　The hour of rest is gone,
And urgent voices, round us, say,
　　"Ho, lingerer, hasten on!"

And has the soul, then, only gained,
　　From this brief time of ease,
A moment's rest, when overstrained,
　　One hurried glimpse of peace?

No; while the sun shone kindly o'er us,
　　And flowers bloomed round our feet, —
While many a bud of joy before us
　　Unclosed its petals sweet, —

An unseen work within was plying;
　　Like honey-seeking bee,
From flower to flower, unwearied, flying,
　　Laboured one faculty, —

Thoughtful for Winter's future sorrow,
　　Its gloom and scarcity;
Prescient to-day, of want to-morrow,
　　Toiled quiet Memory.

'Tis she that from each transient pleasure
　　Extracts a lasting good;
'Tis she that finds, in summer, treasure
　　To serve for winter's food.

And when Youth's summer day is vanished,
　　And Age brings Winter's stress,
Her stores, with hoarded sweets replenished,
　　Life's evening hours will bless.

## On the Death of Emily Jane Brontë

My darling, thou wilt never know
The grinding agony of woe
  That we have borne for thee.
Thus may we consolation tear
E'en from the depth of our despair
  And wasting misery.

The nightly anguish thou art spared
When all the crushing truth is bared
  To the awakening mind,
When the galled heart is pierced with grief,
Till wildly it implores relief,
  But small relief can find.

Nor know'st thou what it is to lie
Looking forth with streaming eye
  On life's lone wilderness.
'Weary, weary, dark and drear,
How shall I the journey bear,
  The burden and distress?'

Then since thou art spared such pain
We will not wish thee here again;
  He that lives must mourn.
God help us through our misery
And give us rest and joy with thee
  When we reach our bourne!

*December* 24, 1848.

## On the Death of Anne Brontë

There's little joy in life for me,
  And little terror in the grave;
I've lived the parting hour to see
  Of one I would have died to save.

Calmly to watch the failing breath,
  Wishing each sigh might be the last;

Longing to see the shade of death
  O'er those belovèd features cast.

The cloud, the stillness that must part
  The darling of my life from me;
And then to thank God from my heart,
  To thank Him well and fervently;

Although I knew that we had lost
  The hope and glory of our life;
And now, benighted, tempest-tossed,
  Must bear alone the weary strife.

           *June* 21, 1849.

# EMILY BRONTË

## Faith and Despondency

"The winter wind is loud and wild,
Come close to me, my darling child;
Forsake thy books, and mateless play;
And, while the night is gathering grey,
We'll talk its pensive hours away; —

"Iernë, round our sheltered hall
November's gusts unheeded call;
Not one faint breath can enter here
Enough to wave my daughter's hair,
And I am glad to watch the blaze
Glance from her eyes, with mimic rays;
To feel her cheek, so softly pressed,
In happy quiet on my breast.

"But, yet, even this tranquillity
Brings bitter, restless thoughts to me;
And, in the red fire's cheerful glow,
I think of deep glens, blocked with snow;
I dream of moor, and misty hill,
Where evening closes dark and chill;
For, lone, among the mountains cold,
Lie those that I have loved of old.
And my heart aches, in hopeless pain
Exhausted with repinings vain,
That I shall greet them ne'er again!"

"Father, in early infancy,
When you were far beyond the sea,
Such thoughts were tyrants over me!
I often sat, for hours together,
Through the long nights of angry weather,
Raised on my pillow, to descry
The dim moon struggling in the sky;
Or, with strained ear, to catch the shock,
Of rock with wave, and wave with rock;
So would I fearful vigil keep,
And, all for listening, never sleep.

But this world's life has much to dread,
Not so, my Father, with the dead.

"Oh! not for them, should we despair,
The grave is drear, but they are not there;
Their dust is mingled with the sod,
Their happy souls are gone to God!
You told me this, and yet you sigh,
And murmur that your friends must die.
Ah! my dear father, tell me why?
For, if your former words were true,
How useless would such sorrow be;
As wise, to mourn the seed which grew
Unnoticed on its parent tree, .
Because it fell in fertile earth,
And sprang up to a glorious birth —
Struck deep its root, and lifted high
Its green boughs, in the breezy sky.

"But, I'll not fear, I will not weep
For those whose bodies rest in sleep, —
I know there is a blessed shore,
    Opening its ports for me, and mine;
And, gazing Time's wide waters o'er,
    I weary for that land divine,
Where we were born, where you and I
Shall meet our Dearest, when we die;
From suffering and corruption free,
Restored into the Deity."

"Well hast thou spoken, sweet, trustful child!
    And wiser than thy sire;
And worldly tempests, raging wild,
    Shall strengthen thy desire —
Thy fervent hope, through storm and foam,
    Through wind and ocean's roar,
To reach, at last, the eternal home,
    The steadfast, changeless, shore!"

# Stars

Ah! why, because the dazzling sun
  Restored our Earth to joy,
Have you departed, every one,
  And left a desert sky?

All through the night, your glorious eyes
  Were gazing down in mine,
And, with a full heart's thankful sighs,
  I blessed that watch divine.

I was at peace, and drank your beams
  As they were life to me;
And revelled in my changeful dreams,
  Like petrel on the sea.

Thought followed thought, star followed star,
  Through boundless regions, on;
While one sweet influence, near and far,
  Thrilled through, and proved us one!

Why did the morning dawn to break
  So great, so pure, a spell;
And scorch with fire, the tranquil cheek,
  Where your cool radiance fell?

Blood-red, he rose, and, arrow-straight,
  His fierce beams struck my brow;
The soul of nature, sprang, elate,
  But *mine* sank sad and low!

My lids closed down, yet through their veil,
  I saw him, blazing, still,
And steep in gold the misty dale,
  And flash upon the hill.

I turned me to the pillow, then,
  To call back night, and see
Your worlds of solemn light, again,
  Throb with my heart, and me!

It would not do — the pillow glowed,
  And glowed both roof and floor;

And birds sang loudly in the wood,
  And fresh winds shook the door;

The curtains waved, the wakened flies
  Were murmuring round my room,
Imprisoned there, till I should rise,
  And give them leave to roam.

Oh, stars, and dreams, and gentle night;
  Oh, night and stars return!
And hide me from the hostile light,
  That does not warm, but burn;

That drains the blood of suffering men;
  Drinks tears, instead of dew;
Let me sleep through his blinding reign,
  And only wake with you!

## The Philosopher

"Enough of thought, philosopher!
  Too long hast thou been dreaming
Unlightened, in this chamber drear,
  While summer's sun is beaming!
Space-sweeping soul, what sad refrain
Concludes thy musings once again?

  "Oh, for the time when I shall sleep
  Without identity,
  And never care how rain may steep,
  Or snow may cover me!
  No promised heaven, these wild desires,
  Could all, or half fulfil;
  No threatened hell, with quenchless fires,
  Subdue this quenchless will!"

"So said I, and still say the same;
  Still, to my death, will say —
Three gods, within this little frame,
  Are warring night and day;

Heaven could not hold them all, and yet
   They all are held in me;
And must be mine till I forget
   My present entity!
Oh, for the time, when in my breast
   Their struggles will be o'er!
Oh, for the day, when I shall rest,
   And never suffer more!"

"I saw a spirit, standing, man,
   Where thou dost stand — an hour ago,
And round his feet three rivers ran,
   Of equal depth, and equal flow —
A golden stream — and one like blood;
   And one like sapphire seemed to be;
But, where they joined their triple flood
   It tumbled in an inky sea.
The spirit sent his dazzling gaze
   Down through that ocean's gloomy night
Then, kindling all, with sudden blaze,
   The glad deep sparkled wide and bright —
White as the sun, far, far more fair
   Than its divided sources were!"

"And even for that spirit, seer,
   I've watched and sought my life-time long;
Sought him in heaven, hell, earth, and air —
   An endless search, and always wrong!
Had I but seen his glorious eye
   *Once* light the clouds that wilder me,
I ne'er had raised this coward cry
   To cease to think, and cease to be;
I ne'er had called oblivion blest,
   Nor, stretching eager hands to death,
Implored to change for senseless rest
   This sentient soul, this living breath —
Oh, let me die — that power and will
   Their cruel strife may close;
And conquered good, and conquering ill
   Be lost in one repose!"

# Remembrance

Cold in the earth — and the deep snow piled above thee,
Far, far, removed, cold in the dreary grave!
Have I forgot, my only Love, to love thee,
Severed at last by Time's all-severing wave?

Now, when alone, do my thoughts no longer hover
Over the mountains, on that northern shore,
Resting their wings where heath and fern-leaves cover
Thy noble heart for ever, ever more?

Cold in the earth — and fifteen wild Decembers,
From those brown hills, have melted into spring:
Faithful, indeed, is the spirit that remembers
After such years of change and suffering!

Sweet Love of youth, forgive, if I forget thee,
While the world's tide is bearing me along;
Other desires and other hopes beset me,
Hopes which obscure, but cannot do thee wrong!

No later light has lightened up my heaven,
No second morn has ever shone for me;
All my life's bliss from thy dear life was given,
All my life's bliss is in the grave with thee.

But, when the days of golden dreams had perished,
And even Despair was powerless to destroy;
Then did I learn how existence could be cherished,
Strengthened, and fed without the aid of joy.

Then did I check the tears of useless passion —
Weaned my young soul from yearning after thine;
Sternly denied its burning wish to hasten
Down to that tomb already more than mine.

And, even yet, I dare not let it languish,
Dare not indulge in memory's rapturous pain;
Once drinking deep of that divinest anguish,
How could I seek the empty world again?

## A Death-Scene

"O Day! he cannot die
When thou so fair art shining!
O Sun, in such a glorious sky,
So tranquilly declining;

He cannot leave thee now,
While fresh west winds are blowing,
And all around his youthful brow
Thy cheerful light is glowing!

Edward, awake, awake —
The golden evening gleams
Warm and bright on Arden's lake —
Arouse thee from thy dreams!

Beside thee, on my knee,
My dearest friend! I pray
That thou, to cross the eternal sea,
Wouldst yet one hour delay:

I hear its billows roar —
I see them foaming high;
But no glimpse of a further shore
Has blest my straining eye.

Believe not what they urge
Of Eden isles beyond;
Turn back, from that tempestuous surge,
To thy own native land.

It is not death, but pain
That struggles in thy breast —
Nay, rally, Edward, rouse again;
I cannot let thee rest!"

One long look, that sore reproved me
For the woe I could not bear —
One mute look of suffering moved me
To repent my useless prayer:

And, with sudden check, the heaving
Of distraction passed away;

Not a sign of further grieving
Stirred my soul that awful day.

Paled, at length, the sweet sun setting;
Sunk to peace the twilight breeze:
Summer dews fell softly, wetting
Glen, and glade, and silent trees.

Then his eyes began to weary,
Weighed beneath a mortal sleep;
And their orbs grew strangely dreary,
Clouded, even as they would weep.

But they wept not, but they changed not,
Never moved, and never closed;
Troubled still, and still they ranged not —
Wandered not, nor yet reposed!

So I knew that he was dying —
Stooped, and raised his languid head;
Felt no breath, and heard no sighing,
So I knew that he was dead.

## Song

The linnet in the rocky dells,
    The moor-lark in the air,
The bee among the heather bells,
    That hide my lady fair:

The wild deer browse above her breast;
    The wild birds raise their brood;
And they, her smiles of love caressed,
    Have left her solitude!

I ween, that when the grave's dark wall
    Did first her form retain;
They thought their hearts could ne'er recall
    The light of joy again.

They thought the tide of grief would flow
    Unchecked through future years;
But where is all their anguish now,
    And where are all their tears?

Well, let them fight for honour's breath,
    Or pleasure's shade pursue —
The dweller in the land of death
    Is changed and careless too.

And, if their eyes should watch and weep
    Till sorrow's source were dry,
She would not, in her tranquil sleep,
    Return a single sigh!

Blow, west-wind, by the lonely mound,
    And murmur, summer-streams —
There is no need of other sound
    To soothe my lady's dreams.

# Anticipation

How beautiful the earth is still,
To thee — how full of happiness!
How little fraught with real ill,
Or unreal phantoms of distress!
How spring can bring thee glory, yet,
And summer win thee to forget
December's sullen time!
Why dost thou hold the treasure fast,
Of youth's delight, when youth is past,
    And thou art near thy prime?

When those who were thy own compeers,
Equals in fortune and in years,
Have seen their morning melt in tears,
    To clouded, smileless day;
Blest, had they died untried and young,
Before their hearts went wandering wrong,
Poor slaves, subdued by passions strong,
    A weak and helpless prey!

"Because, I hoped while they enjoyed,
And, by fulfilment, hope destroyed;
As children hope, with trustful breast,
I waited bliss — and cherished rest.
A thoughtful spirit taught me, soon,
That we must long till life be done;
That every phase of earthly joy
Must always fade, and always cloy:

This I foresaw — and would not chase
    The fleeting treacheries;
But, with firm foot and tranquil face,
Held backward from that tempting race,
Gazed o'er the sands the waves efface,
    To the enduring seas —
There cast my anchor of desire
Deep in unknown eternity;
Nor ever let my spirit tire,
With looking for *what is to be*!

It is hope's spell that glorifies,
Like youth, to my maturer eyes,
All Nature's million mysteries,
    The fearful and the fair —
Hope soothes me in the griefs I know;
She lulls my pain for others' woe,
And makes me strong to undergo
    What I am born to bear.

Glad comforter! will I not brave,
Unawed, the darkness of the grave?
Nay, smile to hear Death's billows rave —
    Sustained, my guide, by thee?
The more unjust seems present fate,
The more my spirit swells elate,
Strong, in thy strength, to anticipate
    Rewarding destiny!"

# The Prisoner

### A FRAGMENT

In the dungeon-crypts, idly did I stray,
Reckless of the lives wasting there away;
"Draw the ponderous bars! open, Warder stern!"
He dared not say me nay — the hinges harshly turn.

"Our guests are darkly lodged," I whisper'd, gazing through
The vault, whose grated eye showed heaven more grey than blue;
(This was when glad spring laughed in awaking pride;)
"Aye, darkly lodged enough!" returned my sullen guide.

Then, God forgive my youth; forgive my careless tongue;
I scoffed, as the chill chains on the damp flag-stones rung:
"Confined in triple walls, art thou so much to fear,
That we must bind thee down and clench thy fetters here?"

The captive raised her face, it was as soft and mild
As sculptured marble saint, or slumbering unwean'd child;
It was so soft and mild, it was so sweet and fair,
Pain could not trace a line, nor grief a shadow there!

The captive raised her hand and pressed it to her brow;
"I have been struck," she said, "and I am suffering now;
Yet these are little worth, your bolts and irons strong,
And, were they forged in steel, they could not hold me long."

Hoarse laughed the jailor grim: "Shall I be won to hear;
Dost think, fond, dreaming wretch, that *I* shall grant thy prayer?
Or, better still, wilt melt my master's heart with groans?
Ah! sooner might the sun thaw down these granite stones.

"My master's voice is low, his aspect bland and kind,
But hard as hardest flint, the soul that lurks behind;
And I am rough and rude, yet not more rough to see
Than is the hidden ghost that has its home in me."

About her lips there played a smile of almost scorn,
"My friend," she gently said, "you have not heard me mourn;
When you my kindred's lives, *my* lost life, can restore,
Then may I weep and sue, — but never, friend, before!

Still, let my tyrants know, I am not doomed to wear
Year after year in gloom, and desolate despair;
A messenger of Hope, comes every night to me,
And offers for short life, eternal liberty.

He comes with western winds, with evening's wandering airs,
With that clear dusk of heaven that brings the thickest stars.
Winds take a pensive tone, and stars a tender fire,
And visions rise, and change, that kill me with desire.

Desire for nothing known in my maturer years,
When Joy grew mad with awe, at counting future tears.
When, if my spirit's sky was full of flashes warm,
I knew not whence they came, from sun, or thunder storm.

But, first, a hush of peace — a soundless calm descends;
The struggle of distress, and fierce impatience ends.
Mute music soothes my breast, unuttered harmony,
That I could never dream, till Earth was lost to me.

Then dawns the Invisible; the Unseen its truth reveals;
My outward sense is gone, my inward essence feels:
Its wings are almost free — its home, its harbour found,
Measuring the gulph, it stoops, and dares the final bound.

Oh, dreadful is the check — intense the agony —
When the ear begins to hear, and the eye begins to see;
When the pulse begins to throb, the brain to think again,
The soul to feel the flesh, and the flesh to feel the chain.

Yet I would lose no sting, would wish no torture less,
The more that anguish racks, the earlier it will bless;
And robed in fires of hell, or bright with heavenly shine,
If it but herald death, the vision is divine!"

She ceased to speak, and we, unanswering, turned to go —
We had no further power to work the captive woe:
Her cheek, her gleaming eye, declared that man had given
A sentence, unapproved, and overruled by Heaven.

## Hope

Hope was but a timid friend;
    She sat without the grated den,
Watching how my fate would tend,
    Even as selfish-hearted men.

She was cruel in her fear;
    Through the bars, one dreary day,
I looked out to see her there,
    And she turned her face away!

Like a false guard, false watch keeping,
    Still, in strife, she whispered peace;
She would sing while I was weeping;
    If I listened, she would cease.

False she was, and unrelenting;
    When my last joys strewed the ground,
Even Sorrow saw, repenting,
    Those sad relics scattered round;

Hope, whose whisper would have given
    Balm to all my frenzied pain,
Stretched her wings, and soared to heaven,
    Went, and ne'er returned again!


## A Day Dream

On a sunny brae, alone I lay
    One summer afternoon;
It was the marriage-time of May
    With her young lover, June.

From her mother's heart, seemed loath to part
    That queen of bridal charms,
But her father smiled on the fairest child
    He ever held in his arms.

The trees did wave their plumy crests,
    The glad birds caroled clear;

And I, of all the wedding guests,
   Was only sullen there!

There was not one, but wished to shun
   My aspect void of cheer;
The very grey rocks, looking on,
   Asked, "What do you do here?"

And I could utter no reply;
   In sooth, I did not know
Why I had brought a clouded eye
   To greet the general glow.

So, resting on a healthy bank,
   I took my heart to me;
And we together sadly sank
   Into a reverie.

We thought, "When winter comes again,
   Where will these bright things be?
All vanished, like a vision vain,
   An unreal mockery!

The birds that now so blithely sing,
   Through deserts, frozen dry,
Poor spectres of the perished spring,
   In famished troops, will fly.

And why should we be glad at all?
   The leaf is hardly green,
Before a token of its fall
   Is on the surface seen!"

Now, whether it were really so,
   I never could be sure;
But as in fit of peevish woe,
   I stretched me on the moor.

A thousand thousand gleaming fires
   Seemed kindling in the air;
A thousand thousand silvery lyres
   Resounded far and near:

Methought, the very breath I breathed
   Was full of sparks divine,
And all my heather-couch was wreathed
   By that celestial shine!

And, while the wide earth echoing rung
   To their strange minstrelsy,
The little glittering spirits sung,
   O seemed to sing, to me.

"O mortal! mortal! let them die;
   Let time and tears destroy,
That we may overflow the sky
   With universal joy!

Let grief distract the sufferer's breast,
   And night obscure his way;
They hasten him to endless rest,
   And everlasting day.

To thee the world is like a tomb,
   A desert's naked shore;
To us, in unimagined bloom,
   It brightens more and more!

And, could we lift the veil, and give
   One brief glimpse to thine eye,
Thou wouldst rejoice for those that live,
   *Because* they live to die."

The music ceased; the noonday dream,
   Like dream of night, withdrew;
But Fancy, still, will sometimes deem
   Her fond creation true.

# To Imagination

When weary with the long day's care,
   And earthly change from pain to pain,
And lost and ready to despair,
   Thy kind voice calls me back again:
Oh, my true friend! I am not lone,
While thou canst speak with such a tone!

So hopeless is the world without;
   The world within I doubly prize;
Thy world, where guile, and hate, and doubt,
   And cold suspicion never rise;
Where thou, and I, and Liberty,
Have undisputed sovereignty.

What matters it, that, all around,
   Danger, and guilt, and darkness lie,
If but within our bosom's bound
   We hold a bright, untroubled sky,
Warm with ten thousand mingled rays
Of suns that know no winter days?

Reason, indeed, may oft complain
   For Nature's sad reality,
And tell the suffering heart, how vain
   Its cherished dreams must always be;
And Truth may rudely trample down
The flowers of Fancy, newly-blown:

But, thou art ever there, to bring
   The hovering vision back, and breathe
New glories o'er the blighted spring,
   And call a lovelier Life from Death,
And whisper, with a voice divine,
Of real worlds, as bright as thine.

I trust not to thy phantom bliss,
   Yet, still, in evening's quiet hour,
With never-failing thankfulness,
   I welcome thee, Benignant Power;
Sure solacer of human cares,
And sweeter hope, when hope despairs!

## How Clear She Shines

How clear she shines! How quietly
  I lie beneath her guardian light;
While heaven and earth are whispering me,
  "To morrow, wake, but, dream to-night."
Yes, Fancy, come, my Fairy love!
  These throbbing temples softly kiss;
And bend my lonely couch above
  And bring me rest, and bring me bliss.

The world is going; dark world, adieu!
  Grim world, conceal thee till the day;
The heart, thou canst not all subdue,
  Must still resist, if thou delay!

Thy love I will not, will not share;
  Thy hatred only wakes a smile;
Thy griefs may wound — thy wrongs may tear,
  But, oh, thy lies shall ne'er beguile!
While gazing on the stars that glow
  Above me, in that stormless sea,
I long to hope that all the woe
  Creation knows, is held in thee!

And this shall be my dream to-night;
  I'll think the heaven of glorious spheres
Is rolling on its course of light
  In endless bliss, through endless years;
I'll think, there's not one world above,
  Far as these straining eyes can see,
Where Wisdom ever laughed at Love,
  Or Virtue crouched to Infamy;

Where, writhing 'neath the strokes of Fate,
  The mangled wretch was forced to smile;
To match his patience 'gainst her hate,
  His heart rebellious all the while.
Where Pleasure still will lead to wrong,
  And helpless Reason warn in vain;
And Truth is weak, and Treachery strong;

And Joy the surest path to Pain;
And Peace, the lethargy of Grief;
   And Hope, a phantom of the soul;
And Life, a labour, void and brief;
   And Death, the despot of the whole!


## Sympathy

There should be no despair for you
   While nightly stars are burning;
While evening pours its silent dew
   And sunshine gilds the morning.
There should be no despair — though tears
   May flow down like a river:
Are not the best beloved of years
   Around your heart for ever?

They weep, you weep, it must be so;
   Winds sigh as you are sighing,
And Winter sheds his grief in snow
   Where Autumn's leaves are lying:
Yet, these revive, and from their fate
   Your fate cannot be parted:
Then, journey on, if not elate,
   Still, *never* broken-hearted!


## Plead for Me

Oh, thy bright eyes must answer now,
When Reason, with a scornful brow,
Is mocking at my overthrow!
Oh, thy sweet tongue must plead for me
And tell, why I have chosen thee!

Stern Reason is to judgment come,
Arrayed in all her forms of gloom:
Wilt thou, my advocate, be dumb?
No, radiant angel, speak and say,
Why I did cast the world away.

Why I have persevered to shun
The common paths that others run,
And on a strange road journeyed on,
Heedless, alike, of wealth and power —
Of glory's wreath and pleasure's flower.

These, once, indeed, seemed Beings Divine;
And they, perchance, heard vows of mine,
And saw my offerings on their shrine;
But, careless gifts are seldom prized,
And *mine* were worthily despised.

So, with a ready heart I swore
To seek their altar-stone no more;
And gave my spirit to adore
Thee, ever-present, phantom thing;
My slave, my comrade, and my king,

A slave, because I rule thee still;
Incline thee to my changeful will,
And make thy influence good or ill:
A comrade, for by day and night
Thou art my intimate delight, —

My darling pain that wounds and sears
And wrings a blessing out from tears
By deadening me to earthly cares;
And yet, a king, though Prudence well
Have taught thy subject to rebel.

And am I wrong to worship, where
Faith cannot doubt, nor hope despair,
Since my own soul can grant my prayer?
Speak, God of visions, plead for me,
And tell why I have chosen thee!

## Self-Interrogation

"The evening passes fast away,
   'Tis almost time to rest;
What thoughts has left the vanished day,
   What feelings, in thy breast?

"The vanished day? It leaves a sense
   Of labour hardly done;
Of little, gained with vast expense, —
   A sense of grief alone!

"Time stands before the door of Death,
   Upbraiding bitterly;
And Conscience, with exhaustless breath,
   Pours black reproach on me:

"And though I've said that Conscience lies,
   And Time should Fate condemn;
Still, sad Repentance clouds my eyes,
   And makes me yield to them!

"Then art thou glad to seek repose?
   Art glad to leave the sea,
And anchor all thy weary woes
   In calm Eternity?

"Nothing regrets to see thee go —
   Not one voice sobs 'farewell,'
And where thy heart has suffered so,
   Canst thou desire to dwell?"

"Alas! The countless links are strong
   That bind us to our clay;
The loving spirit lingers long,
   And would not pass away!

"And rest is sweet, when laurelled fame
   Will crown the soldier's crest;
But, a brave heart, with a tarnished name,
   Would rather fight than rest."

"Well, thou hast fought for many a year,
   Hast fought thy whole life through,

Hast humbled Falsehood, trampled Fear;
    What is there left to do?"

" 'Tis true, this arm has hotly striven,
    Has dared what few would dare;
Much have I done, and freely given,
    But little learnt to bear!"

"Look on the grave, where thou must sleep,
    Thy last, and strongest foe;
It is endurance not to weep,
    If that repose seem woe.

"The long war closing in defeat,
    Defeat serenely borne,
Thy midnight rest may still be sweet,
    And break in glorious morn!"

# Death

Death! that struck when I was most confiding
In my certain faith of joy to be —
Strike again, Time's withered branch dividing
From the fresh root of Eternity!

Leaves, upon Time's branch, were growing brightly,
Full of sap, and full of silver dew;
Birds beneath its shelter gathered nightly;
Daily round its flowers the wild bees flew.

Sorrow passed, and plucked the golden blossom;
Guilt stripped off the foliage in its pride;
But, within its parent's kindly bosom,
Flowed for ever Life's restoring tide.

Little mourned I for the parted gladness,
For the vacant nest and silent song —
Hope was there, and laughed me out of sadness;
Whispering, "Winter will not linger long!"

And, behold! with tenfold increase blessing,
Spring adorned the beauty-burdened spray;
Wind and rain and fervent heat, caressing,
Lavished glory on that second May!

High it rose — no winged grief could sweep it;
Sin was scared to distance with its shine;
Love, and its own life, had power to keep it
From all wrong — from every blight but thine!

Cruel Death! The young leaves droop and languish;
Evening's gentle air may still restore —
No! the morning sunshine mocks my anguish —
Time, for me, must never blossom more!

Strike it down, that other boughs may flourish
Where that perished sapling used to be;
Thus, at least, its mouldering corpse will nourish
That from which it sprung — Eternity.

## Stanzas to ——

Well, some may hate, and some may scorn,
And some may quite forget thy name;
But my sad heart must ever mourn
Thy ruined hopes, thy blighted fame!
'Twas thus I thought, an hour ago,
Even weeping o'er that wretch's woe;
One word turned back my gushing tears,
And lit my altered eye with sneers.
Then "Bless the friendly dust," I said,
"That hides thy unlamented head!
Vain as thou wert, and weak as vain,
The slave of Falsehood, Pride, and Pain, —
My heart has nought akin to thine;
Thy soul is powerless over mine."

But these were thoughts that vanished too;
Unwise, unholy, and untrue:
Do I despise the timid deer,
Because his limbs are fleet with fear?

Or, would I mock the wolf's death-howl,
Because his form is gaunt and foul?
Or, hear with joy the leveret's cry,
Because it cannot bravely die?
No! Then above his memory
Let Pity's heart as tender be;
Say, "Earth, lie lightly on that breast,
And, kind Heaven, grant that spirit rest!"

## Stanzas

I'll not weep that thou art going to leave me,
    There's nothing lovely here;
And doubly will the dark world grieve me,
    While thy heart suffers there.

I'll not weep, because the summer's glory
    Must always end in gloom;
And, follow out the happiest story —
    It closes with a tomb!

And I am weary of the anguish
    Increasing winters bear;
Weary to watch the spirit languish
    Through years of dead despair.

So, if a tear, when thou art dying,
    Should haply fall from me,
It is but that my soul is sighing,
    To go and rest with thee.

## My Comforter

Well hast thou spoken, and yet, not taught
    A feeling strange or new;
Thou hast but roused a latent thought,
A cloud-closed beam of sunshine, brought
    To gleam in open view.

Deep down, concealed within my soul,
   That light lies hid from men;
Yet, glows unquenched — though shadows roll,
Its gentle ray cannot control,
   About the sullen den.

Was I not vexed, in these gloomy ways
   To walk alone so long?
Around me, wretches uttering praise,
Or howling o'er their hopeless days,
   And each with Frenzy's tongue; —

A brotherhood of misery,
   Their smiles as sad as sighs;
Whose madness daily maddened me,
Distorting into agony
   The bliss before my eyes!

So stood I, in Heaven's glorious sun,
   And in the glare of Hell;
My spirit drank a mingled tone,
Of seraph's song, and demon's moan;
What my soul bore, my soul alone
   Within itself may tell!

Like a soft air, above a sea,
   Tossed by the tempest's stir;
A thaw-wind, melting quietly
The snow-drift, on some wintry lea;
No: what sweet thing resembles thee,
   My thoughtful Comforter?

And yet a little longer speak,
   Calm this resentful mood;
And while the savage heart grows meek,
For other token do not seek,
But let the tear upon my cheek
   Evince my gratitude!

## The Old Stoic

Riches I hold in light esteem;
    And Love I laugh to scorn;
And lust of fame was but a dream
    That vanished with the morn:

And if I pray, the only prayer
    That moves my lips for me
Is, "Leave the heart that now I bear,
    And give me liberty!"

Yes, as my swift days near their goal,
    'Tis all that I implore;
In life and death, a chainless soul,
    With courage to endure.

## The Visionary[1]

Silent is the house: all are laid asleep;
One, alone, looks out o'er the snow wreaths deep;
Watching every cloud, dreading every breeze
That whirls the wildering drift, and bends the groaning trees.

Cheerful is the hearth, soft the matted floor;
Not one shivering gust creeps through pane or door;
The little lamp burns straight, its rays shoot strong and far;
I trim it well to be the Wanderer's guiding-star.

Frown, my haughty sire; chide, my angry dame;
Set your slaves to spy, threaten me with shame:
But neither sire nor dame, nor prying serf shall know
What angel nightly tracks that waste of frozen snow.

What I love shall come like visitant of air,
Safe in secret power from lurking human snare;

---

[1] The first 12 lines are by Emily from her long narrative poem "Julian M. and A. G. Rochelle" and the last 8 lines were written by Charlotte. This poem was published as "The Visionary" by Emily Brontë in *Wuthering Heights and Agnes Grey* (1850).

Who loves me, no word of mine shall e'er betray,
Though for faith unstained my life must forfeit pay.

Burn, then, little lamp; glimmer straight and clear —
Hush! a rustling wing stirs, methinks, the air:
He for whom I wait, thus ever comes to me;
Strange Power! I trust thy might; trust thou my constancy.

## The Night-Wind

In summer's mellow midnight,
A cloudless moon shone through
Our open parlour window
And rosetrees wet with dew.

I sat in silent musing,
The soft wind waved my hair:
It told me Heaven was glorious,
And sleeping Earth was fair.

I needed not its breathing
To bring such thoughts to me,
But still it whispered lowly,
"How dark the woods will be!

"The thick leaves in my murmur
Are rustling like a dream,
And all their myriad voices
Instinct with spirit seem."

I said, "Go, gentle singer,
Thy wooing voice is kind,
But do not think its music
Has power to reach my mind.

"Play with the scented flower,
The young tree's supple bough,
And leave my human feelings
In their own course to flow."

The wanderer would not leave[1] me;
Its kiss grew warmer still —

---

[1] Or "heed."

"O come," it sighed so sweetly,
"I'll win thee 'gainst thy will.

"Have we not been from childhood friends?
Have I not loved thee long?
As long as thou hast loved the night
Whose silence wakes my song.

"And when thy heart is laid at rest
Beneath the church-yard stone
I shall have time enough to mourn
And thou to be alone."

## No Coward Soul Is Mine

No coward soul is mine
No trembler in the world's storm-troubled sphere
I see Heaven's glories shine
And Faith shines equal arming me from Fear

O God within my breast
Almighty ever-present Deity
Life, that in me hast rest
As I Undying Life, have power in Thee

Vain are the thousand creeds
That move men's hearts, unutterably vain,
Worthless as withered weeds
Or idlest froth amid the boundless main

To waken doubt in one
Holding so fast by thy infinity
So surely anchored on
The steadfast rock of Immortality

With wide-embracing love
Thy spirit animates eternal years
Pervades and broods above,
Changes, sustains, dissolves, creates and rears

Though Earth and moon were gone
And suns and universes ceased to be
And thou wert left alone
Every Existence would exist in thee

There is not room for Death
Nor atom that his might could render void
Since thou art Being and Breath
And what thou art may never be destroyed.

# ANNE BRONTË

## A Reminiscence

Yes, thou art gone! and never more
Thy sunny smile shall gladden me;
But I may pass the old church door,
And pace the floor that covers thee,

May stand upon the cold, damp stone,
And think that, frozen, lies below
The lightest heart that I have known,
The kindest I shall ever know.

Yet, though I cannot see thee more,
'Tis still a comfort to have seen;
And though thy transient life is o'er,
'Tis sweet to think that thou hast been;

To think a soul so near divine,
Within a form, so angel fair,
United to a heart like thine,
Has gladdened once our humble sphere.

## The Arbour

I'll rest me in this sheltered bower,
And look upon the clear blue sky
That smiles upon me through the trees,
Which stand so thickly clustering by;

And view their green and glossy leaves,
All glistening in the sunshine fair;
And list the rustling of their boughs,
So softly whispering through the air.

And while my ear drinks in the sound,
My winged soul shall fly away;
Reviewing long departed years
As one mild, beaming, autumn day;

And soaring on to future scenes,
Like hills and woods, and valleys green,
All basking in the summer's sun,
But distant still, and dimly seen.

Oh, list! 'tis summer's very breath
That gently shakes the rustling trees —
But look! the snow is on the ground —
How can I think of scenes like these?

'Tis but the *frost* that clears the air,
And gives the sky that lovely blue;
They're smiling in a *winter's* sun,
Those evergreens of sombre hue.

And winter's chill is on my heart —
How can I dream of future bliss?
How can my spirit soar away,
Confined by such a chain as this?

## Home

How brightly glistening in the sun
    The woodland ivy plays!
While yonder beeches from their barks
    Reflect his silver rays.

That sun surveys a lovely scene
    From softly smiling skies;
And wildly through unnumbered trees
    The wind of winter sighs:

Now loud, it thunders o'er my head,
    And now in distance dies.
But give me back my barren hills
    Where colder breezes rise;

Where scarce the scattered, stunted trees
    Can yield an answering swell,

But where a wilderness of heath
  Returns the sound as well.

For yonder garden, fair and wide,
  With groves of evergreen,
Long winding walks, and borders trim,
  And velvet lawns between;

Restore to me that little spot,
  With grey walls compassed round,
Where knotted grass neglected lies,
  And weeds usurp the ground.

Though all around this mansion high
  Invites the foot to roam,
And though its halls are fair within —
  Oh, give me back my HOME!

## The Penitent

I mourn with thee, and yet rejoice
  That thou shouldst sorrow so;
With angel choirs I join my voice
  To bless the sinner's woe.

Though friends and kindred turn away,
  And laugh thy grief to scorn;
I hear the great Redeemer say,
  "Blessed are ye that mourn."

Hold on thy course, nor deem it strange
  That earthly cords are riven:
Man may lament the wondrous change,
  But "there is joy in heaven!"

# If This Be All

O God! if this indeed be all
    That Life can show to me;
If on my aching brow may fall
    No freshening dew from Thee, —

If with no brighter light than this
    The lamp of hope may glow,
And I may only *dream* of bliss,
    And wake to weary woe;

If friendship's solace must decay,
    When other joys are gone,
And love must keep so far away,
    While I go wandering on, —

Wandering and toiling without gain,
    The slave of others' will,
With constant care, and frequent pain,
    Despised, forgotten still;

Grieving to look on vice and sin,
    Yet powerless to quell
The silent current from within,
    The outward torrent's swell:

While all the good I would impart,
    The feelings I would share,
Are driven backward to my heart,
    And turned to wormwood, there;

If clouds must *ever* keep from sight
    The glories of the Sun,
And I must suffer Winter's blight,
    Ere Summer is begun;

If Life must be so full of care,
    Then call me soon to Thee;
Or give me strength enough to bear
    My load of misery.

# Memory

Brightly the sun of summer shone,
Green fields and waving woods upon,
   And soft winds wandered by;
Above, a sky of purest blue,
Around, bright flowers of loveliest hue,
   Allured the gazer's eye.

But what were all these charms to me,
When one sweet breath of memory
   Came gently wafting by?
I closed my eyes against the day,
And called my willing soul away,
   From earth, and air, and sky;

That I might simply fancy there
One little flower — a primrose fair,
   Just opening into sight;
As in the days of infancy,
An opening primrose seemed to me
   A source of strange delight.

Sweet Memory! ever smile on me;
Nature's chief beauties spring from thee;
   Oh, still thy tribute bring!
Still make the golden crocus shine
Among the flowers the most divine,
   The glory of the spring.

Still in the wall-flower's fragrance dwell;
And hover round the slight blue bell,
   My childhood's darling flower.
Smile on the little daisy still,
The buttercup's bright goblet fill
   With all thy former power.

For ever hang thy dreamy spell
Round mountain star and heather bell,
   And do not pass away
From sparkling frost, or wreathed snow,
And whisper when the wild winds blow,
   Or rippling waters play.

Is childhood, then, so all divine?
Or Memory, is the glory thine,
    That haloes thus the past?
Not *all* divine; its pangs of grief,
(Although, perchance, their stay be brief,)
    Are bitter while they last.

Nor is the glory all thine own,
For on our earliest joys alone
    That holy light is cast.
With such a ray, no spell of thine
Can make our later pleasures shine,
    Though long ago they passed.


## Past Days

'Tis strange to think, there *was* a time
When mirth was not an empty name,
When laughter really cheered the heart,
And frequent smiles unbidden came,
And tears of grief would only flow
In sympathy for others' woe;

When speech expressed the inward thought,
And heart to kindred heart was bare,
And Summer days were far too short
For all the pleasures crowded there,
And silence, solitude, and rest,
Now welcome to the weary breast —

Were all unprized, uncourted then —
And all the joy one spirit showed,
The other deeply felt again;
And friendship like a river flowed,
Constant and strong its silent course,
For nought withstood its gentle force:

When night, the holy time of peace,
Was dreaded as the parting hour;
When speech and mirth at once must cease,
And Silence must resume her power;

Though ever free from pains and woes,
She only brought us calm repose.

And when the blessed dawn again
Brought daylight to the blushing skies,
We woke, and not *reluctant* then,
To joyless *labour* did we rise;
But full of hope, and glad and gay,
We welcomed the returning day.

## Lines Composed in a Wood on a Windy Day

My soul is awakened, my spirit is soaring
And carried aloft on the wings of the breeze;
For above and around me the wild wind is roaring,
Arousing to rapture the earth and the seas.

The long withered grass in the sunshine is glancing,
The bare trees are tossing their branches on high;
The dead leaves, beneath them, are merrily dancing,
The white clouds are scudding across the blue sky.

I wish I could see how the ocean is lashing
The foam of its billows to whirlwinds of spray;
I wish I could see how its proud waves are dashing,
And hear the wild roar of their thunder to-day!

## Appeal

Oh, I am very weary,
    Though tears no longer flow;
My eyes are tired of weeping,
    My heart is sick of woe;

My life is very lonely,
    My days pass heavily,
I'm weary of repining,
    Wilt thou not come to me?

Oh, didst thou know my longings
   For thee, from day to day,
My hopes, so often blighted,
   Thou wouldst not thus delay!


## The Captive Dove

Poor restless dove, I pity thee;
And when I hear thy plaintive moan,
I mourn for thy captivity,
And in thy woes forget mine own.

To see thee stand prepared to fly,
And flap those useless wings of thine,
And gaze into the distant sky,
Would melt a harder heart than mine.

In vain — in vain! Thou canst not rise:
Thy prison roof confines thee there;
Its slender wires delude thine eyes,
And quench thy longings with despair.

Oh, thou wert made to wander free
In sunny mead and shady grove,
And, far beyond the rolling sea,
In distant climes, at will to rove!

Yet, hadst thou but one gentle mate
Thy little drooping heart to cheer,
And share with thee thy captive state,
Thou couldst be happy even there.

Yes, even there, if, listening by,
One faithful dear companion stood,
While gazing on her full bright eye,
Thou mightst forget thy native wood.

But thou, poor solitary dove,
  Must make, unheard, thy joyless moan;
The heart, that Nature formed to love,
  Must pine, neglected, and alone.


## Self-Congratulation

Ellen, you were thoughtless once
  Of beauty or of grace,
Simple and homely in attire,
  Careless of form and face;
Then whence this change? and wherefore now
  So often smooth your hair?
And wherefore deck your youthful form
  With such unwearied care?

Tell us — and cease to tire our ears
  With that familiar strain —
Why will you play those simple tunes
  So often, o'er again?
"Indeed, dear friends, I can but say
  That childhood's thoughts are gone;
Each year its own new feelings brings,
  And years move swiftly on:

"And for these little simple airs —
  I love to play them o'er
So much — I dare not promise, now,
  To play them never more."
I answered — and it was enough;
  They turned them to depart;
They could not read my secret thoughts,
  Nor see my throbbing heart.

I've noticed many a youthful form,
  Upon whose changeful face
The inmost workings of the soul
  The gazer well might trace;
The speaking eye, the changing lip,
  The ready blushing cheek,

The smiling, or beclouded brow,
    Their different feelings speak.

But, thank God! you might gaze on mine
    For hours, and never know
The secret changes of my soul
    From joy to keenest woe.
Last night, as we sat round the fire
    Conversing merrily,
We heard, without, approaching steps
    Of one well known to me!

There was no trembling in my voice,
    No blush upon my cheek,
No lustrous sparkle in my eyes,
    Of hope, or joy, to speak;
But, oh! my spirit burned within,
    My heart beat full and fast!
He came not nigh — he went away —
    And then my joy was past.

And yet my comrades marked it not:
    My voice was still the same;
They saw me smile, and o'er my face
    No signs of sadness came.
They little knew my hidden thoughts;
    And they will *never* know
The aching anguish of my heart,
    The bitter burning woe!

## Fluctuations

What though the Sun had left my sky;
    To save me from despair
The blessed Moon arose on high,
    And shone serenely there.

I watched her, with a tearful gaze,
    Rise slowly o'er the hill,
While through the dim horizon's haze
    Her light gleamed faint and chill.

I thought such wan and lifeless beams
  Could ne'er my heart repay,
For the bright sun's most transient gleams
  That cheered me through the day:

But as above that mist's control
  She rose, and brighter shone,
I felt her light upon my soul;
  But now — that light is gone!

Thick vapours snatched her from my sight,
  And I was darkling left,
All in the cold and gloomy night,
  Of light and hope bereft:

Until, methought, a little star
  Shone forth with trembling ray,
To cheer me with its light afar —
  But that, too, passed away.

Anon, an earthly meteor blazed
  The gloomy darkness through;
I smiled, yet trembled while I gazed —
  But that soon vanished too!

And darker, drearier fell the night
  Upon my spirit then; —
But what is that faint struggling light?
  Is it the Moon again?

Kind Heaven! increase that silvery gleam,
  And bid these clouds depart,
And let her soft celestial beam
  Restore my fainting heart!

## The Bluebell

A fine and subtle spirit dwells
  In every little flower,
Each one its own sweet feeling breathes
  With more or less of power.

There is a silent eloquence
  In every wild bluebell,
That fills my softened heart with bliss
  That words could never tell.

Yet I recall, not long ago,
  A bright and sunny day:
'Twas when I led a toilsome life
  So many leagues away.

That day along a sunny road
  All carelessly I strayed
Between two banks where smiling flowers
  Their varied hues displayed.

Before me rose a lofty hill,
  Behind me lay the sea;
My heart was not so heavy then
  As it was wont to be.

Less harassed than at other times
  I saw the scene was fair,
And spoke and laughed to those around,
  As if I knew no care.

But as I looked upon the bank,
  My wandering glances fell
Upon a little trembling flower,
  A single sweet bluebell.

Whence came that rising in my throat,
  That dimness in my eyes?
Why did those burning drops distil,
  Those bitter feelings rise?

Oh, that lone flower recalled to me
  My happy childhood's hours,
When bluebells seemed like fairy gifts,
  A prize among the flowers.

Those sunny days of merriment
  When heart and soul were free,

And when I dwelt with kindred hearts
   That loved and cared for me.

I had not then mid heartless crowds
   To spend a thankless life,
In seeking after others' weal
   With anxious toil and strife.

'Sad wanderer, weep those blissful times
   That never may return!'
The lovely floweret seemed to say,
   And thus it made me mourn.


## Last Lines

I hoped, that with the brave and strong,
   My portioned task might lie;
To toil amid the busy throng,
   With purpose pure and high.

But God has fixed another part,
   And He has fixed it well;
I said so with my bleeding heart,
   When first the anguish fell.

A dreadful darkness closes in
   On my bewildered mind;
Oh, let me suffer and not sin,
   Be tortured, yet resigned.

Shall I with joy thy blessings share
   And not endure their loss?
Or hope the martyr's crown to wear
   And cast away the cross?

Thou, God, hast taken our delight,[1]
   Our treasured hope away;

---

[1] Emily Jane Brontë, who had died on December 19, 1848, a few weeks before this poem was written.

Thou bidst us now weep through the night
  And sorrow through the day.

These weary hours will not be lost,
  These days of misery,
These nights of darkness, anguish-tost,
  Can I but turn to Thee.

Weak and weary though I lie,
  Crushed with sorrow, worn with pain,
I may lift to Heaven mine eye,
  And strive to labour not in vain;

That inward strife against the sins
  That ever wait on suffering
To strike whatever first begins:
  Each ill that would corruption bring;

That secret labour to sustain
  With humble patience every blow;
To gather fortitude from pain,
  And hope and holiness from woe.

Thus let me serve Thee from my heart,
  Whate'er may be my written fate:
Whether thus early to depart,
  Or yet a while to wait.

If thou shouldst bring me back to life,
  More humbled I should be;
More wise, more strengthened for the strife,
  More apt to lean on Thee.

Should death be standing at the gate,
  Thus should I keep my vow;
But, Lord! whatever be my fate,
  Oh, let me serve Thee now!

'These lines written, the desk was closed, the pen laid aside — for ever.' — *Note by Charlotte Brontë.*